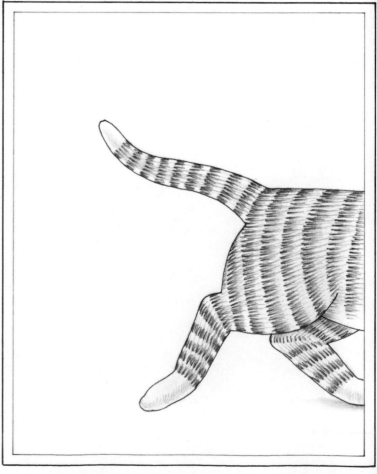

CATS' EYES

ANTHONY TABER

Thomas Congdon Books

E.P. DUTTON · NEW YORK

FOR MARIANN

This is Tiger.

REMEMBERING

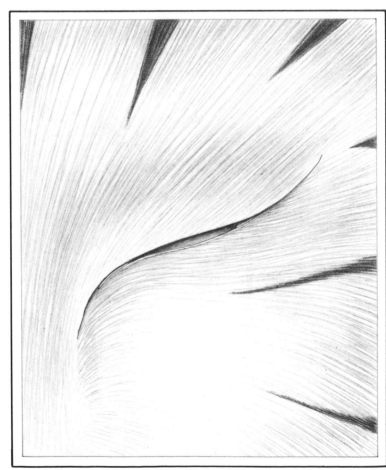

His first home was
our living room closet.
Two weeks after his birth,
Tiger opened his eyes.

FIRST LOOK

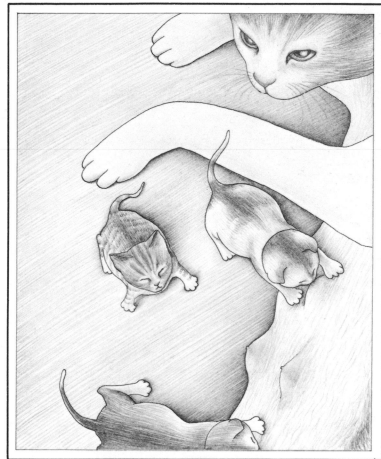

Tiger's mom was named Gypsy.
She adopted us shortly before
she had her litter.

MOM

In the beginning,
the kittens drank a lot of milk,
tried to crawl, got bathed,
lay around snoozing and grew bigger.

IN THE NEST...

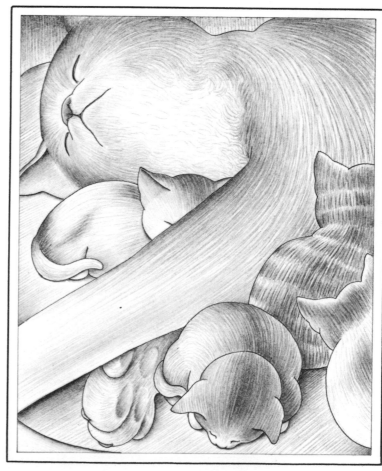

One day Tiger started wondering
what was beyond the closet door.

AND BEYOND

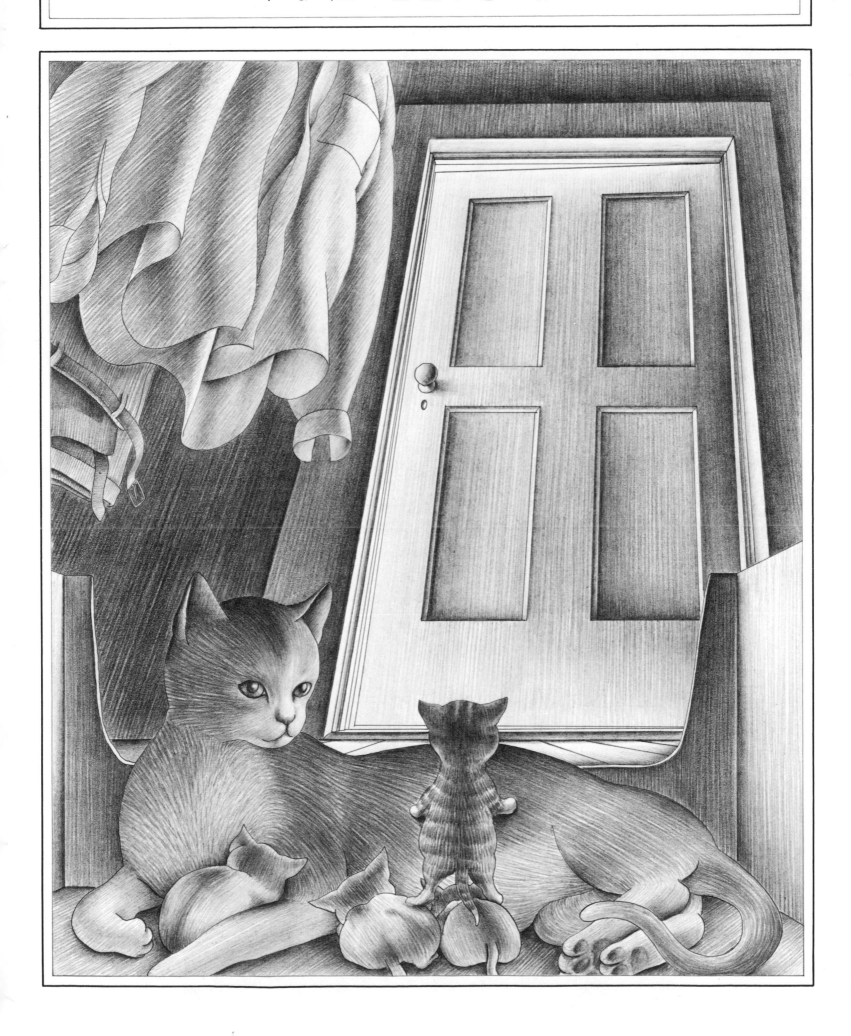

FIRST TIME OUT...

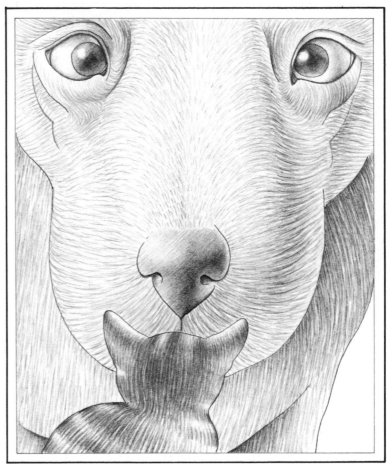

That was George, our big gentle dog.

This is Mariann.

Everyday she stopped in to say hello.

VISITOR

One day the kittens woke up
to find the door wide open.

SECOND TIME OUT

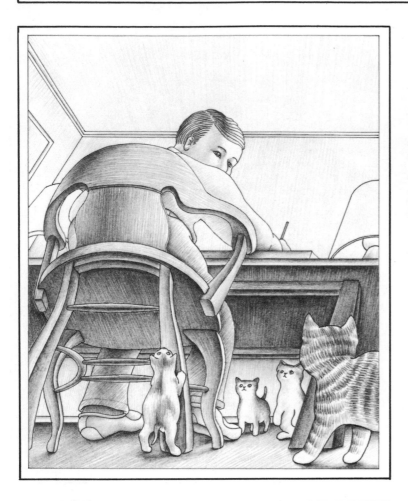

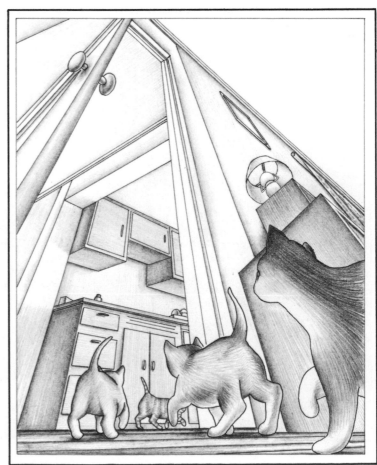

NEW TERRITORY

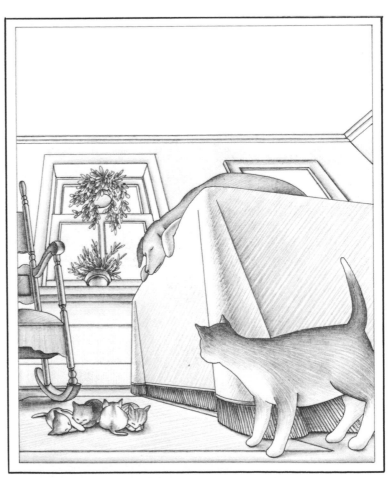

In the many days that followed
they learned marvelous things,
like claws and how to use them.

LEARNING NEW SKILLS

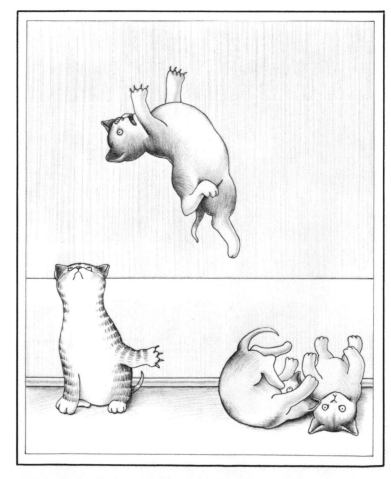

CLIMBING

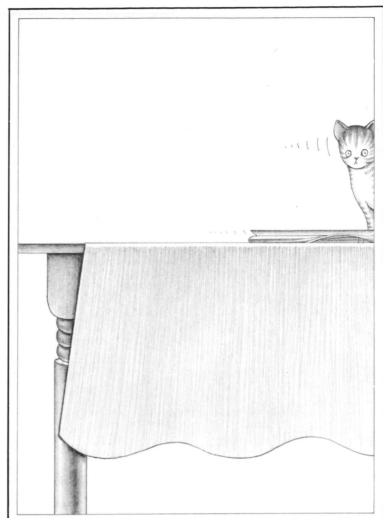

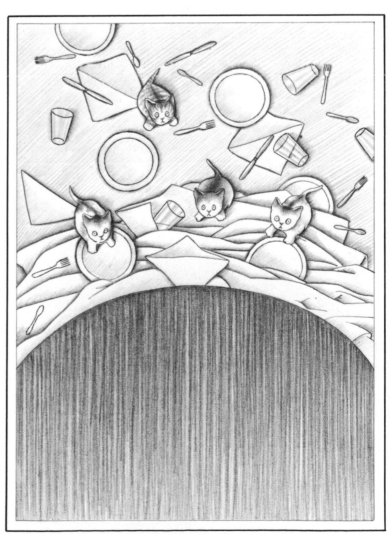

and …

HUNTING PRACTICE

LEARNING HOW TO DRINK

Drinking was easy compared
to learning how to eat.

TRYING TO EAT

Then George helped out.

EATING

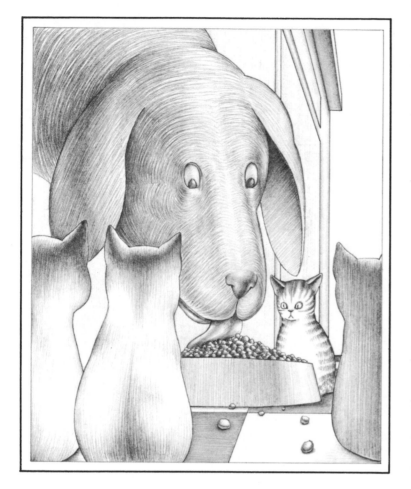

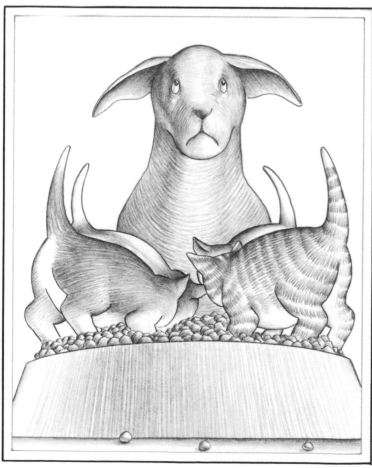

Mom tried to help too.

EATING BETTER

Then came human beings.
It didn't take long to figure out
how useful and amusing they were.

HUMANS

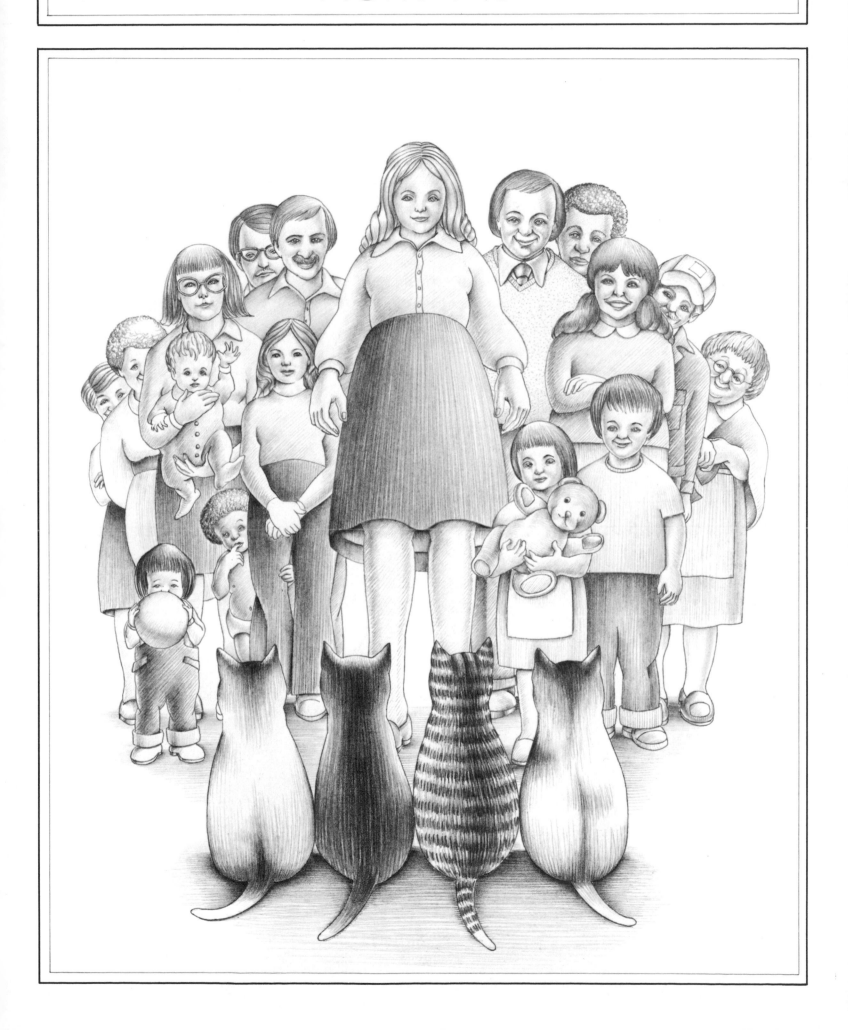

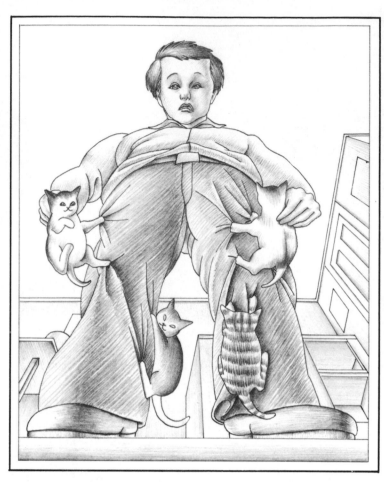

Best of all …

All that love and food made
the kittens larger and larger.

GETTING BIGGER

Now they were big enough
to go outside.

GOING OUTSIDE

Outside meant many new adventures.

MORE HUNTING PRACTICE

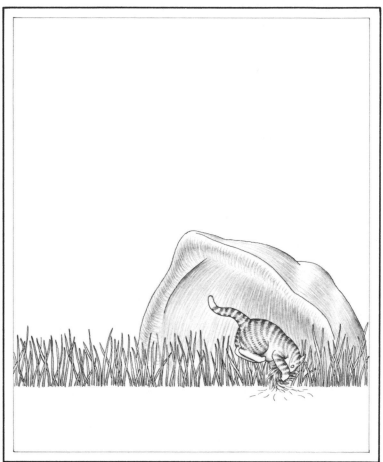

CHASING...

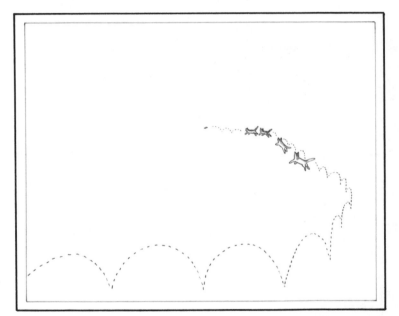

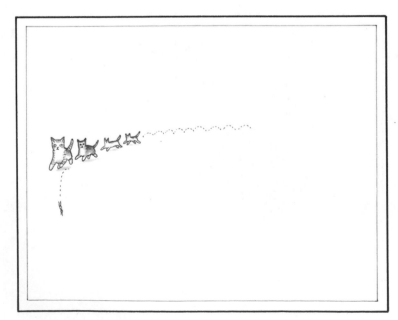

AND BEING CHASED

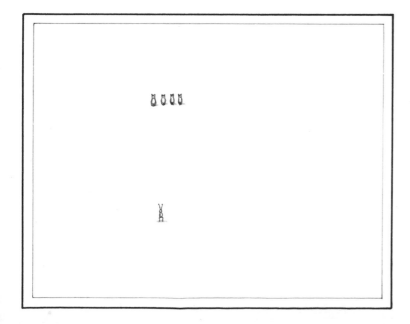

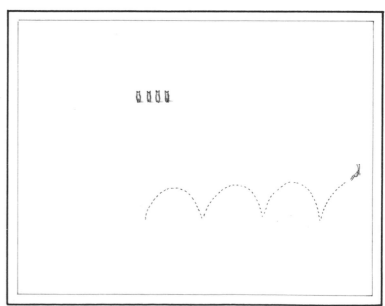

When Gypsy's family was grown,
we found a larger home for them
on a nearby farm.
The people were kind and there was
plenty of mice and milk.
But Tiger didn't want to leave Mariann,
so he stayed at our house.

NEW HOME

As a young adult,
Tiger was ready to mate.
It took a little while to figure out
what he was supposed to do.

"HER," AND THE COMPETITION

But having understood, he did well.

MARRIAGE

Very well indeed!!

NEW FAMILY

Tiger finally learned how to hunt.

REAL HUNTING

Because his favorite pastime
was finding food,
Tiger got big and fat,
but just being fed at home was boring
compared to scavenging and
begging and stealing.

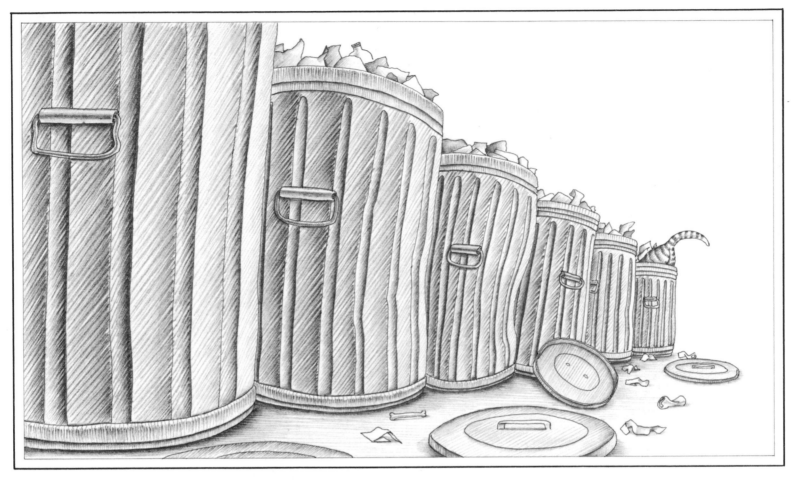

Outside of fathering kittens
and scrounging food,
Tiger's pleasures were few and simple
but so thoroughly enjoyable
he never tired of them.

FAVORITE PASTIMES

In his later years,
Tiger spent a lot of time watching,
listening and just being still.

BEING OLD

On his last day,
Tiger came and stayed with Mariann
the whole morning and after getting
a last pat, quietly went outside
to his favorite tree.
Mariann didn't know he
had said good-bye.

FAREWELL

 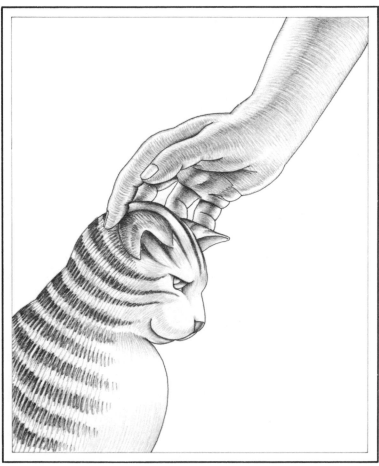

Tiger felt very happy and peaceful.

FINAL LOOK

His mind was filled with
happy memories.

REMEMBERING

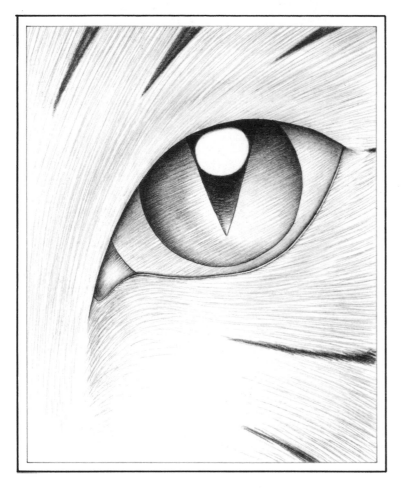

Very drowsy,
he lay down and went to sleep.

LAST NAP

It was sad to say good-bye.

MOURNING

But Tiger had left a lot of himself
around the countryside.

MEETING...

He didn't let Mariann
be sad for long.

A NEW FRIEND

ABOUT THE AUTHOR

Anthony Taber started drawing for
The New Yorker at the age of nineteen.
He has also been published in *Esquire,
Saturday Review, Better Homes*
and the *New York Times*.
He is a graduate of the
Philadelphia College of Art and now
lives in Ithaca, New York.